AF322678

ON-TIME

Written by Candace McIntosh-Pond, MA, LMFT and Brian Pond, MA, PPS

Illustrated by Funda May

Robinson lost track of time and stayed up too late playing video game.

His mom tries to wake him up, but he won't get out of bed. Instead, he covers his head. His father comes in the room and says, "Robinson you're sleeping in, is going to make us all late."

Robinson runs down the stairs as quick as he can. He has no time for breakfast because he is already late.

As he runs to class he is stopped and given a late pass.

Robinson opens the classroom door just as his teacher Mrs. Frans says, "Close your reading books, it's time for Math."

Robinson is sad because he missed his favorite part of the day, his reading class. "Aw Man!"

Mom and dad received a letter in the mail. The school is requesting their presence. The school counselor wants to meet about getting to school on time.

SCHOOL

The school counselor, Robinson and his parents meet to discuss the barriers to Robinson getting to school on time.

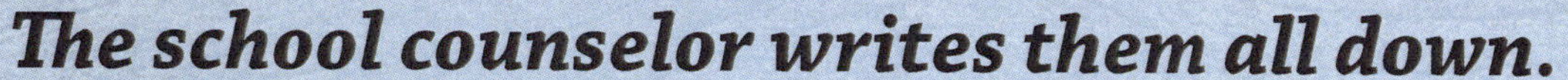

The school counselor writes them all down.

Go to bed on-time
Have grandma drive Robinson to school
Get to school 30 mins early for breakfast
Set an alarm clock to wake up on time
Get ready for school the night before

The school counselor suggested ways for Robinson to get to school on time with the help of his parents.

Robinson was so excited about his new plan to get to school on time. He called and asked his grandmother to take him to school in the morning.

Grandma said "of course!"

1- All electronic devices turned off at 6:00pm.

2- Get clothes and backpack ready the night before.

3- Set an alarm clock to wake up on time.

4- Go to bed on time.
5- Have grandma drive to school.
6- Get to school 15-30 minutes early.
SCHOOL
SCHOOL

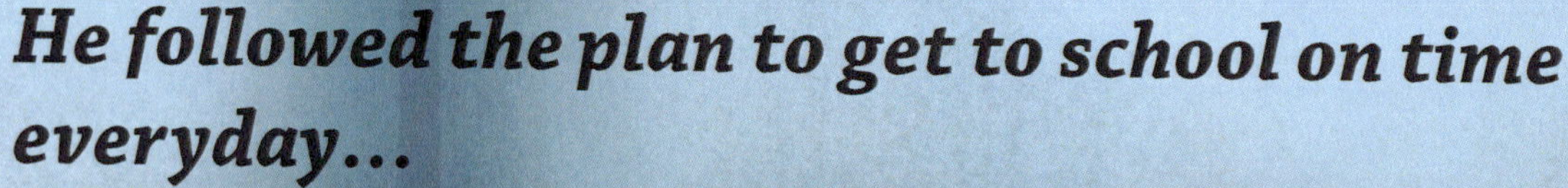

He followed the plan to get to school on time everyday…

IT WORKED!!! Robinson received a reward for being ON TIME. He was so proud of himself. He was able to follow the plan.